The Vent: Book Deux

W9-BGW-433

yes, you've done it again

In the autumn of 1995, we gathered together the best of the AJC's popular daily feature, The Vent, and turned it into a bestselling book. Overjoyed at our ability to successfully traffic in the nameless brilliance of others, we considered the critical issue confronting all successful marketers: How can we ride this horse until it drops dead?

Hence, **The Vent: Book Deux.**

You, the readers of The Atlanta Journal-Constitution, did all the work on this sequel, of course. You jammed our Vent line with hundreds of calls a day. You built a series of anonymous messages into a tome. Some might even say an epi-tome: a 162-page tribute to your own wit, frustration and bent observations.

We would like to send each of you a check, but we are unable to pierce the veil of your treasured anonymity and so must reluctantly become the financial guardians of the fruits of your labor.

Thanks for everything. May your venting be unrelenting.

who's responsible for this?

Joey Ledford, whose true identity as the Vent Guy may now be revealed — but only to people who paid hard currency for this book — edited this volume.

Richard Halicks, a former Vent Guy now on parole, changed a bunch of Joey's stuff and designed and produced the book.

Hyde Post put Joey's stuff back in and changed a bunch of Richard's stuff and was, as ever, in charge of the whole enterprise.

Ron Martin, editor of The Atlanta Journal-Constitution, has gamely tolerated the Vent and its strange and militant adherents on the staff.

John Amoss, creator of the frightening Vent phone illustration, created a bunch more of them for this second effort. He also did the cover.

ConVentional *Wisdom*

In Alabama, ATF
— Alcohol, Tobacco and Firearms —
isn't a government agency.
It's a shopping list for the weekend.

When I get down about my life,
I just think to myself, "At least I'm not O.J."

The only thing I have going for me right now
is that I might already be a winner.

Hello, is this AT&T? Hello? I can't hear you.
You're breaking up.

All my life I've been sowing my wild oats,
and now I'm praying for a crop failure.

I'm going to stay up all night tonight
and call the gas company.

It's a dog-eat-dog world
and I'm wearing milkbone shorts.

I can't find my car keys.
I think I left them in my car,
which was stolen last Thursday.

Never pull a shirt

over your head

with a cigarette

in your mouth.

A friend asked me if I wanted to go fishing and I said, "Get real, man. You can buy fish."

We need to find out where Colin Campbell is going on vacation so we can warn them.

This is to the blind guy who sat out
the hurricane in the nude outside his apartment.
I want to party with you, dude.

I'm a factory owner and I love working
my employees for nothing and mistreating them.
I really enjoy that.

Every time a bell rings, an angel gets his wings.
And everytime the microwave beeps,
I get a hot burrito.

If the end of the world comes,
I hope to be in Alabama, because
everything happens there 20 years later.

I paid my county property tax
and now I think I'm pregnant.

I don't use direct deposit because my paycheck
is too little to get to the bank by itself.

Instead of that irritating tone you get
when you forget to dial the area code,
the phone company should just have
Homer Simpson say, "Doh!"

If man evolved from monkeys and apes,
then why do we still have monkeys and apes?
Shouldn't they be extinct by now?

I love Lucy, but I dream of Jeannie.

I love Lucy, I dream of Jeannie,
but I'm married to Roseanne.

If you want breakfast in bed, sleep in the kitchen.

Thou shalt not weigh more than the refrigerator.

My wife makes me clean the house
before the cleaning lady comes.

It would be the best TV show ever if all the guys
on "ER" and all the guys on "Friends"
got together and went to a Braves game.

Friends don't let friends
watch "Friends."

A job application asked,
"Who do we call in case of an emergency?"
I put, "The Vent."

On my job application for who to call
in case of an emergency, I put "911."

I was filling out a job application
and where it said sex, I wrote,
"One time on top of Stone Mountain."

If there are many more new talk shows
on TV, there won't be anybody left
to work at the Waffle House.

My cellular phone dropped every call yesterday.
I guess I had a bad air day.

You know it's going to be a bad day
when you turn on the news and see your house.

I guess I have a redneck family, too.
I was mowing the grass and came upon a car.

I went to college with a set of identical twins
and one of them was ugly.

Sometimes I wake up grouchy
and other times I let him sleep late.

I got the mushroom treatment at work.
First I was kept in the dark,
then they covered me with manure.
Today, I got canned.

If at first you don't succeed,
find out if the loser gets anything.

Irony is when you buy a suit
with two pair of pants
and then burn a hole in the coat.

Yes, I miss Alabama too. I drive west
and the first thing I know, I'm in Mississippi.

I filled out a credit card application
and it asked for my nearest relative.
I put 47 miles. Do you think that's too far?

My bathroom caught on fire last night,
but we put it out before it reached the house.

I read so much about the evils
of drinking and smoking
that I've given up reading.

There is a fine line between

fishing and standing

on the shore like an idiot.

Ventricles: *Affairs of the heart*

Nothing makes my day better than a
sexy country boy waving to me
from a big old 4 x 4 truck.

My husband took off his shirt and sat down.
I suddenly realized I was married to Yoda.

My girlfriend told me she was Satan's concubine.
Should I be worried?

I had a good wife,
but her husband came and took her home.

The problem with men and women dating
is that women are looking for Mr. Right
and men are looking for Ms. Right Now.

My wife said she wanted something crazy
and expensive for Christmas that she doesn't really
need, so I signed her up for radiation treatments.

I was married by a judge,
but I believe I should have asked for a jury.

My girlfriend called and said,
"I'm pregnant, but I don't think it's mine."

Married people don't

live longer than single people.

It just seems longer.

My wife and I plan to conceive
a baby on April 1, 1999.

I called my wife at work and told her how much
I loved her and enjoyed sleeping with her
and she said, "Who's calling, please?"

I asked my wife, "I don't look 46, do I?"
She said, "No, but you used to."

Two weeks ago, my ex-girlfriend moved to Tampa
and took my dog with her. Three days after
she got there, the dog ran away.
Last night, when I got home from work,
he was asleep on my porch.
God, I love that dog.

My boyfriend's name is Moses
and it fits him very well because
every time he opens his mouth, the bull rushes.

I asked my dad how I will know if I'm truly successful. He said, "Your wife will tell you."

Nine out of 10 men who have tried Camels prefer women.

I am thinking about marrying my cousin Jason.

Why does it seem the only women I meet
are blondes trapped in brunettes' bodies?

My girlfriend and I broke up.
She wanted to get married and I didn't want her to.

My wife said if I don't give up golf,
she is going to leave me. Darn, I'm going to miss her.

To the guy whose dog barks at him when he comes
back from out of town travel, but wags his tail
for his best friend: Do you have a wife?

Hey, guys out there: I'm not that kind of girl,
but I could be.

My wife called and said,
"You dirty old man.
You got me pregnant."
I said, "Who is this?"

I'm married and I keep getting calls from singles club. Do you think they know something I don't?

Is my husband the only man in the world who has to have his boxer shorts sewn up in the front?

Can I borrow Chipper Jones for one night?

I'm so tired of my wife acting like she never has gas.

I have a tent and a BMW
and now I only need one good man.

I lost my wife and my dog.
I'm offering a $100 reward for the dog.

My wife always called people who lived
in mobile homes "Spam-sucking trailer trash."
Since our divorce, she has lived in a trailer.
So I sent her a can of Spam with a note that said,
"Food for thought."

When I ask a girl to dance and she says no, I say,
"You must be mistaken.
I said you look fat in those pants."

When you are turned down for a date, say,
"Don't be picky. I wasn't."

I'm really getting old. Last night, I went to my wife
and told her I was having an affair.
She looked me in the eye and asked,
"Who's catering it?"

I must be the luckiest guy in the world.
My wife treats me like a god.
Every meal she serves me is a burnt offering.

When you wear one of those cute windbreaker outfits,
you look like a big trash bag.

I told my wife I needed more space,
so she locked me outside.

I married a moonshiner's daughter
and I love her still.

Try to get married in the morning.
That way, if it doesn't work out,
you haven't wasted a whole day.

I told my wife that Wednesday was hump day,
but that didn't work, either.

I want to buck up, kick back and father
Lotta Mae's love child.

Men like to put me up on a pedestal
and then look up my dress.

When a man takes Midol, I can describe
what happens in two words — Dennis Rodman.

I confess. I'm a guy who used to take Midol,
but I had to stop. I forgot how to parallel park
and I began saying things like hemstitch
and casserole and go to the mall.

Why is it that when a women turns 40,
the body parts that used to get her a date
now get her a doctor's appointment?

Marriage is when a man agrees to spend
the rest of his life sleeping in a room
that is too hot beside a woman who is sleeping
in a room that is too cold.

I was married once. Now I just lease.

The more I watch Ricki Lake,
the better my husband looks.

Ventilation *Therapy*

I got a happy meal today and it didn't work.

I saw this sign at the zoo: "Please do not feed the animals. If you have any suitable food, give it to the guard on duty."

For sale: Parachute. Never opened. Small stain.

I only need four hours of sleep at night. I sleep fast.

Hukt on fonix wurkd four me.

Editorials are just long vents that aren't even funny.

My boss said, "You should have been here at 8."
I said, "Why, what happened?"

When a fly lands on the ceiling, does it
fly upside down or does it just flip over
at the last second?

What I want to know is, why are the Martians throwing rocks at us? They sure have a rotten aim, too, hitting Antarctica.

I am Mark from Mars, and I want my rock back.

Life on Mars? Big deal. Haven't you people ever heard of the Klingons, the Romulans and the Vulcans?

Woody Harrelson planted four pot seeds, and was charged with a misdemeanor. If he had planted five, it would have been a felony. It is obvious the government has this drug thing under control.

Did you see that Timothy Leary went to the University of Alabama? I guess that's why he always said, "Tune in, turn on, drop out, Roll Tide."

The Vent proves one thing:

We are all ignorant,

but on different subjects.

The Braves win the World Series.
Atlanta gets the Olympics.
The Falcons win the Super Bowl.
. . . Sorry, lost it there for a minute.

The reason you see so many obese people
in the grocery store is because
that's where the food is.

Could someone get some chairs
for all those operators who are always standing by?

I just got all my wisdom teeth cut out
and it really, really hurt.

Last time I checked the drugs worked OK.

I hate cooking fried chicken without a shirt on.

Research has shown that every four seconds
a woman gives birth to a baby.
We must find this woman and stop her!

Coming home, I drove to the wrong house
and collided with a tree I don't have.

There are three kinds
of people in this world
— those who can count and those who can't.

When someone says, "Have a nice day,"
tell them you have other plans.

When Glenn Burns draws the Cash 3,
why do the people who are there to certify it
walk off the stage before he's done?

The first time I walked
into a trophy shop,
I said to myself,
"Boy, this guy is good."

Some guy must think I'm a weatherman.
The phone rang last night and before
I could say anything he wanted to know
if the coast was clear.

The Information Superhighway
is just one really big Vent.

I just learned my bank is broke.
They just sent back my checks marked
"Insufficient Funds." And I thought they had
plenty of money.

Suggested title for the next Vent book:
"They Vent That a Vay."

Never go to a doctor whose office plants have died.

My wooden dummy and I read the Vent together.

You know you are losing it when you
pick up your remote and try to
use it like a calculator.

I can't decide if I want to go back to the future
or go forward to the pasture.

Watch out, I'm wearing boxer shorts
and I know how to use them.

I work in the hospital and I would like for all
the patients to know you need to keep
your underpants on, even when
you have on a gown.

I think there was a serious divorce in Henry County today. I noticed one-half of a double-wide trailer sitting on the side of I-75 with nobody pulling it.

My boss won't tolerate tardiness.
A co-worker came limping in 30 minutes late,
saying he fell down a flight of stairs.
My boss said, "Don't tell me it took you 30
minutes to fall down a flight of stairs."

Only users lose drugs.

Generation *Vent*

My daughter's cat died. I told her,
"Cabbie is in heaven now."
She replied,
"What does God want with a dead cat?"

When I die, I want to go like grandpa did,
quietly in his sleep;
not screaming like the passengers in his car.

When my dad gets old, he says he wants
to be the person at Wal-Mart
who gives people their carts.

I'm 80 years old today, can't see or hear,
but thank God I can still drive.

I just called my mother to tell her
I tripped over my cat, cut myself
and had to get three stitches.
She asked me if the cat was OK.

You know it's going to be a bad day
when you step out of bed and mortally wound
your child's runaway hamster.

My mother is a

travel agent for guilt trips.

You know you're a loser when you
find yourself cheating while playing Candy Land
with your 5-year-old son.

When I was young, I used to stop by the drug store
to get condoms and after shave lotion.
Now I stop there to get Tums and Doan's pills.

I promised my son $50 if he would not smoke until after he was 16. He did it, and we had a family ceremony. He spent it on liquor.

I have reached the age where I no longer buy the newspaper to read the articles. The main reason I use it now is to keep track of the day of the week.

If my parents are couch potatoes, does that make me a tater tot?

We retired in the suburbs near the kids
and they promptly moved away.

My father always told me that blackberries
are red when they are green.

You know you're getting old when Scope
tastes better than scotch.

I got lost on the way to my grandmother's house,
so I asked for directions and the guy said,
"Over the river and through the woods."

I slept in and my 6-year-old girl brought me
my favorite coffee cup. I looked inside
and there were three Army soldiers.
I said, "Honey, what is this?"
She said, "Mommy, the best part of waking up
is soldiers in your cup."

At one point I was an out-of-control teenager.
I didn't really enjoy being one;
I was just trying to keep up with my friends.

I wish parents would spend as much time
teaching their children manners
as they do picking out their Nintendo games.

School will start soon

and the bus drivers

will have all their problems

behind them.

I'm 70 years old and I want to be a topless dancer.

I was doing 70 on I-85 and I got passed by a hearse.
Was the guy in back late for something?

Mommy, when we run low on orange juice,
don't add water to it, because we know.

I have no idea why they are called Generation X.
I'm a baby boomer and my kids
keep coming back.
I call them baby boomerangs.

First you wanted me to stay a child
as long as possible. Now that I'm 22
you want me to grow up. You are confusing me.

You know you are really getting old
when your hair turns white.

I have white hair,
and just because there is snow on the roof
doesn't mean there isn't fire in the furnace.

I believe in keeping our country safe
for our children, but not our children's children,
because children shouldn't have sex.

I watched a talk show and they said,
"If you are 15 years old and gay, and your parents
won't accept it, you can be a guest on this show.
Call this number." And then they said,
"You must be 18 or older to call."

I went to Jenny Craig and lost 20 pounds,
bought Oil of Olay for my skin,
Dove for my face
and some hair extender
and then my class reunion was canceled.

We have to get sex education out of the schools
and back into cars where it belongs.

They say that age is only a number,
but I prefer to keep mine unlisted.

What, no Pink Pig? I grew up with him
and I want my children to grow up with him.
I want my children's children to grow up with him.
Bring back the pig!

Do you know what I just found out today?
My parents were married on the same day!

Freedom is when the children leave home
and the dog dies.

My wife wanted to call our daughter Sue,
but I felt that in our family
that was usually a verb.

Kids are expensive,

but they do last a long time.

My parents are coming in on Friday
and we haven't seen them in a while.
Think they would mind babysitting
while we go to a party?

Why is it that it is almost impossible to get a child
in the bathtub, then once you get them there,
it is almost impossible to get them out?

Hey Mom, I have been accepted
at the Glenn Burns weather school.

I erected a steel beam, built my mailbox around it
and the neighborhood teenager
with his baseball bat
vibrated for three months.

Most kids do chores for their allowance.
At my house, I guess you could call it
more like a modern-day welfare program.

After my 6-year-old was tripped and hurt at school,
he turned to the boy who tripped him and said,
"This is going to be a stain in your life
that will never come out."

My father was a truck driver,
but now he is semi-retired.

I lost my job, and my daughter said
I should call the Vent.
I said, "Why, are they hiring?"

Vent *on* **Wheels**

This is to the lady with the "God is My Co-Pilot"
bumper sticker who ran two of us off the road:
Next time let God drive.

If I have been diagnosed with multiple personalities,
will I be able to use the HOV lane?

When I drive around on the interstates in Atlanta,
I stay within the speed limit and try to obey
all the traffic laws, because, you see,
I drive around in the nude
and I sure don't want to get caught doing that.

What's yellow and sleeps six? A DOT truck.

What was the State Patrol doing before they started enforcing the speed limit?

The State Patrol was eating doughnuts and reading the Vent until you dummies told them how fast we were going.

The person who complained about me
running red lights should understand that
I am a very important person
and am not bound by your silly laws.

This is to the idiot in front of us in the HOV lane.
Just because everyone in the other lanes is doing 35
doesn't mean you have to.
There is no one in front of you.

I saw a sign in Cartersville that said,
"This ditch owned and maintained by Ga. DOT."
How do you maintain a ditch?

Yes, Atlanta, it's possible
— I got a ticket for not using my blinker.

Now that the HOV lanes are done,
can we beat the stuffing out of Ed from the DOT?

If the junction of I-85 and 285 is Spaghetti Junction,
then the junction of 285 and I-75
should be Linguine Junction.

I was sitting in traffic the other day trying
to figure out why. I looked up and a big
DOT sign told me: "Traffic is moving slowly."

When traffic's going good, I wish the DOT would throw
some Vents up on those big new highway signs.

The DOT says the new cameras on the expressway
will give drivers more intelligent choices.
I would like to know what choices
do you really have in gridlock?

Atlanta should be called
"The City of Brake Lights."

What is more annoying, the guy who doesn't
signal lane changes or the guy who does
and leaves his signal on for five miles?

Cobb County drivers are a hazard.
COBB stands for Can't Operate Brakes or Blinkers.

I have to admit the Georgia State Patrol's crackdown
on interstate speeders is working.
People who used to pass me going 90
are now only doing 75.

If a hearse is carrying a body,
can the driver use the HOV lane?

I agree, Atlanta drivers should slow down
and take time to smell the fumes.

Speeding never kills. It's those sudden stops.

The DOT should put up a big sign that says,
"If you are from out-of-town, drive your butt
around the city instead of through it, so the people
who live here can get where they are going."

It's too bad the DOT was not around
when Sherman invaded.
They could have stopped him cold.

I feel like a true Atlantan now.
I was just in my first multi-car wreck.

I rear-ended a car yesterday. I told the policeman
it was all my fault. I told him the lady signaled left,
then turned left. That was so unusual,
I wasn't used to that.

I think the new narrow expressway lanes are
unsafe, stressful, risky, dangerous, absurd,
a hazard, chancy and ridiculous.
Other than that they're OK.

When the DOT finishes narrowing the lanes,
I can share my Grey Poupon
with drivers on each side of my car.

How come nobody on 75 north stopped
and picked me up when I had my thumb out
and a gas can in my hand? Did you think I was
going to rob you with a gas can?

Today I raced my sports car against a mini-van
and I lost.

I got pulled over in Atlanta by a cop
for going 75 mph. I told him it wasn't fair,
because I'd only been out for 15 minutes.

You can't drive with your high beams on
just because one of your low beams is burned out.

Someone please remind me what those
DOT flashing signs are supposed to do,
since I have yet to see one working
that is not warning us of traffic on the Connector
we're already in.

The flashing light in the upper right corner
of the multi-million dollar traffic sign
means the batteries are low.

vent on wheels / III

The guy was all over the road!
I had to swerve a number of times before I hit him.

Is there something wrong with the right lane
on the interstate? Nobody ever uses it but me.
It is kind of nice, though,
because I can go real fast over there.

Ventennial
Games

Frankly, Mr. Samaranch, I don't give a damn what you thought about the Olympics.

To Kerri Strug: I loved you in "The Wizard of Oz."

I had a dream last night that I was
Alexi Niemov's pommel horse.

All the world is a stage,
but not everyone can get tickets.

Who says Olympics tickets are hard to get?
I found a scalper who sold me tickets to the downhill
and the luge — at face value!

As the line moved toward and through the entrance
of Centennial Olympic Park, a female voice repeated
over and over on the speaker:
"Please have all your zippers unzipped
so we can check the contents."

That blue line is actually where Bubba and Earl dragged Izzy out of town.

What a moving moment when Muhammad Ali
lit the Olympic caldron. But wouldn't it have been
more dramatic to shoot a flaming Izzy from a cannon?

Have you heard the secret plan
for the Opening Ceremony? Someone is going
to hurl a flaming possum over the unlit torch.

You know the Olympics are in town when
you are going the speed limit in Stone Mountain
and get passed by a gang of women on bicycles.

I say we crank up those chrome pickup trucks
and go out and kick ourselves some terrorist butt.

If Charles Barkley is on the U.S. basketball team,
why isn't Hulk Hogan on the U.S. wrestling team?

Remember the train ride in Dr. Zhivago?
The downtown employee shuttles are worse.

The strange route the torch took through all
the small areas of Atlanta was determined
by following a taxicab from the airport to downtown.

Ha ha to everyone who really thought
they were going to get $1,000 a day for their houses.

If the parade of athletes is removed from the
Opening Ceremony, as has been suggested,
would it be replaced by the more meaningful
and appropriate parade of Olympic sponsors?

If there is one thing Sydney should learn,
it's to suck up to the press.

What do you get when

2 million Olympic visitors

flush at the same time?

ACLOG.

So many more snide comments to be made
about ACOG and so little time.

Folks, you don't need your Olympic credentials
to get into Kroger.

Attention all ACOG volunteers:
Take your MARTA card off your neck chain
before inserting card into slot at the station.

Tonight I broke my toe racing for the phone.
I was afraid if I didn't answer by the fifth ring,
ACOG would sue me.

Sometimes, when I'm eating my Cheerios,
groups of five form the Olympic rings.

I'm no prude, but I think the women's volleyball shorts are about half a cheek too small.

If the 81st-ranked player was the best the U.S. could muster for the Olympic table tennis competition, why didn't we enter Forrest Gump?

As a native Atlantan, we do not want the world
to come here. In fact, we want the people
who have come here in the last 30 years
to go back home.

We had 8 million visitors? Who counted them?

There once was a city near here,
That invited the world to appear.
The world came and went,
Watching every event,
And construction was done the next year.

When the Olympics are over, can we use the
countdown sign for something really important,
like college football?

Buy a brick and get laid in the park.

That big blue thing in Centennial Park
— I think that's Izzy's mother.

Microchips were attached to shoes in some
Olympic running events to assure accurate timing.
I guess that means:
"These are the soles that timed men's tries."

My wife says why don't we rent our house
for the Olympics and just live in a hotel room.
Is she a genius, or what?

In downtown Atlanta,

the shortest distance

between two points

is under construction.

State *of the* **Vent**

Should I vote for Clinton the dummy
or Dole the mummy?

Bob Dole wants our kids to grow up like he did.
Personally, I want my kids
to have electricity and indoor plumbing.

One thing about cold weather: It makes it easier
to see if Bob Dole is breathing.

Ross Perot should quit eating so much British beef.
It's beginning to show.

If I vent at least 50 times, do I get a tote bag?

I like those self-adhesive postage stamps,
but I hated putting one that said "love" on my
income tax envelope. Doesn't the post office
have one with a snake or something?

I go into the post office every day
just to point out which one is most likely to snap.

Do you have to pay state and federal income taxe
on embezzled money?

Shame on The AJC: You published a picture
Sunday of Newt with a rhinoceros
and you didn't tell us which was which.

In the rhino picture,
Newt is the one with the horns.

It looks like the choice Americans
have for president in November is between
the codger and the dodger.

If Bob Dole is our "grandfather" candidate,
would that make Pat Buchanan
our "grand wizard" candidate?

We all know how the judicial system works
in this country now. A man is definitely innocent
until he runs out of attorney's fees.

The judge and the police are all in cahoots,
except one wears a robe and the others wear boots.

Excuse me, could you spare a little social change?

If you are innocent until proven guilty,
why are you locked up
until you're proven innocent?

Hey judge, shouldn't we have two search warrants:
one for the suspect's house
and one for the cop's car to make sure
they didn't steal anything
from the suspect's house?

I believe that primitive man invented
warfare and capitalism to avoid child care.

I'm suing the city of Atlanta.
I went on my bike to report someone stealing my car.
When I left the police station,
my bike was gone.

Thoroughly **H**apless **E**ccentrics
Voicing **E**xcessively **N**eurotic **T**hemes.

Is Jimmy Carter the Susan Lucci of geopolitics?

People usually get what's coming to them
— unless it's been mailed.

Does anyone know the difference between the
House of Representatives and the Boy Scouts?
The Boy Scouts have adult leadership.

From the moment I picked the Vent book
up to the moment I put it down
I was convulsed with laughter.
One day I will read it.

Some people are all bent out of shape
because the French are testing their nuclear weapons.
Think about it. Do you want a bunch
of untested nuclear weapons lying around?

It's time to do away with the electric chair.
What we need now are electric bleachers.

Would you send your sons to Cobb County
to fight for human rights?

The other day I heard a guy talking on a cell phone
while sitting in a bathroom stall.

When the helmet law is repealed, they can
change the name from motorcycle to donorcycle.

Every time I play my losing Lotto numbers,
I know Zell Miller feels my pain.

The Georgia Lottery is a tax
on people who are bad at math.

If God had intended

people to vote,

he would have given us

some candidates.

Questionable *Vent*

I wonder how much deeper the ocean
would be if sponges did not live there?

Am I the only one who thinks if you flash
the CNN logo into the sky,
Ted Turner would show up?

If a product causes cancer is California,
doesn't that mean we are OK in Georgia?

If Calvin Klein is a genius,
what does that make Michael Jackson?

If all streets were one-way,
which way would you go?

Have you ever asked yourself why
the big steam carpet cleaners send some
ex-con dirt bag to clean your carpet
and not the guy on TV?

Why speak your mind,
when a finger says so much?

If you were to be cremated and your remains
put in an urn and the urn was a music box,
what tune would you have it play?

A group vent: "Dust in the Wind";
"How Dry I Am"; "Always and Forever";
"Come Play in the Dirt Again";
"Smoke Gets in Your Eyes"; "Stairway to Heaven";
"There Has Been a Change in Me";
"Another One Bites the Dust";
and "something from the Grateful Dead."

I just read the Lotto jackpot for Saturday
would pay $9 million for a single winner.
How much would a married winner get?

Why didn't I win that $87 million Powerball jackpot?
I would have shared.

If you put a Slinky

on an escalator,

will it go forever?

I told my wife it was time to rotate
the tires on her car. She said,
"Don't they rotate when I drive?"

How can you live in Newnan
and not need a drink?

Could someone please tell me how to get
the Georgia clay stains off my dog?

My snap, crackle and pop cereal
doesn't have any life to it lately.
Is there a cereal killer on the loose?

My cat just lost her rabies tag.
Should I put a Post-it on her rear end
saying lost tag?

Does voluntary manslaughter mean
the victim said it was OK?

So, what was the final pollen count?

So when can we expect the Monkees' Anthology?

Why do the MARTA trains stop between
stations and just sit there?

Why is it that anal-retentive readers
insist on answering rhetorical questions?

When you have leftovers, is that deja food?

Would someone please send me
an 8x10 glossy of the big picture?

My 3-year-old just asked me why
the itsy bitsy spider went back up the water spout.
Anybody know?

The itsy bitsy spider climbed back up the spout
because that's his web site.
Just ask him at www.itsy.bitsy.com.

I see my vents in the book,

but how do I know

I called them in?